Patchwork

Patchwork

Seminole and Miccosukee Art and Activities

Dorothy Downs

Pineapple Press
Sarasota, Florida

Inquiries should be addressed to:

Pineapple Press, Inc.
P.O. Box 3889
Sarasota, Florida 34230

www.pineapplepress.com

Library of Congress Cataloging-in-Publication Data

Downs, Dorothy, 1937-
  Patchwork : seminole and miccosukee art and activities / Dorothy Downs.-- 1st
ed.
      p. cm.
  ISBN 1-56164-332-7 (alk. paper)
  1. Patchwork--Florida--Juvenile literature. 2. Seminole art--Florida--Juvenile
literature. 3. Mikasuki art--Florida--Juvenile literature. I. Title.
  TT835.D712 2005
  746.46'08997'3859--dc22

                                                              2005009272

ISBN-13: 978-1-56164-332-5

Note:
Pineapple Press books are available at special quantity discounts to use as
premiums or promotions or for use in training programs. For more information,
write to Director of Special Sales, Pineapple Press, P.O. Box 3889, Sarasota, FL
34230. Or call 800-746-3275. Or contact your local bookseller.

First Edition
10 9 8 7 6 5 4 3 2

Design by Shé Hicks
Printed in China

For ages 9–12

Table of Contents

Introduction
Seminoles and Miccosukees

The **Seminole** Tribe of Florida was officially recognized by the United States government in 1957. Approximately 1600 people are now registered members of the tribe. Their south Florida headquarters are on the Hollywood **reservation**. (A reservation is land set aside for the people by the United States government or land the tribes have purchased.) Tribal members living on the Hollywood, Big Cypress, Immokalee, and the smaller Tampa and Ft. Pierce reservations speak the **Mikasuki** language. Seminoles living on the Brighton reservation speak the Muskogee, or Creek, language.

The **Miccosukee** Tribe of Indians of Florida was incorporated in 1962. At that time, leaders changed the spelling of the name for their people and the language they speak from Mikasuki to "Miccosukee," to distinguish their new tribe. The people live on their reservation where tribal offices are located. The reservation is west of Miami along Highway US 41, also known as the Tamiami Trail, near the Shark Valley entrance to the Everglades National

Park. Reservation land is also set aside along the section of I-75 known as Alligator Alley. They have businesses on that reservation, but they do not live there. Over 500 people are registered members of the Miccosukee tribe.

Some south Florida Native Americans choose not to belong to either tribe and do not live on a reservation.

◆ 1 ◆
Patchwork
Clothes as Art

You may not realize that the clothes that you wear can be considered art. Surprised? Art is not just painted pictures to hang on the walls or sculpture to touch or walk around. All people, from prehistoric times to modern times, have created art, one way or another. Anything that someone creates using skills and imagination can be art: the print of a hand carefully placed on the wall, a basket woven of grasses, a quilt, or a ceramic pot. Why not a shoulder bag, shirt, or skirt?

You can learn a lot about the Florida Seminole and Miccosukee Indians from their clothes and accessories. Accessories are things like jewelry, scarves, and belts worn with clothes. These Native Americans wear their art! The finest art of many Native American people is found in the clothes and accessories that they create. The Seminoles and Miccosukees are best known for their colorful **patchwork** clothing.

If you see an old photo of a Native American man wearing a patchwork outfit in a dugout canoe, do you know that he used his canoe to hunt and fish in the Florida Everglades? He was a Seminole or Miccosukee Indian and he lived in a **chickee**, an open-sided house with a palmetto-thatched roof. Each group of Native Americans is very different from the others. Where they live affects what they eat, the kind of house they live in, the things that they believe, how they dress, and the art they create.

Chickees

A chickee is an open-sided house with a roof made of palmetto fronds. Of all Native American tribes, only the Seminoles and Miccosukees of south Florida lived in chickees. Several clan-related families once lived in a camp that had many chickees built on higher ground. The grandmother owned the camp, and her daughters and their families and her unmarried sons lived in the camp too. When a man married, he moved into his wife's family's camp.

A chickee has only one big room. Four posts of cypress support each corner of the roof, the roof frame, and a raised wooden platform built to keep the family safe from snakes and other animals. The palmetto-thatched roof that reaches 12 or more feet above ground is watertight and can even withstand the strong winds of a hurricane.

During the day, the mother sewed clothing for the family on her sewing machine in the chickee. At night, each family slept together on blankets on the platform. Cloth coverings were pulled down on the sides for privacy and protection from mosquitoes and other insects.

The camp had a cooking chickee, where all of the women cooked meals for their families over a wood fire built on the ground in the center of the chickee. The logs of the fire were arranged facing the four directions: east, north, west, and south. A big black pot full of **sofke**, a warm corn drink, simmered over the fire. Shelves built around the sides of the cooking chickee held pots, pans, tin cups and plates, and food supplies.

Men wore a knee length "plain shirt" and a coat called a "long shirt." It also became known as a "doctor's coat" because it was often worn by a medicine man. This was worn with a **turban** on the head and other accessories, such as belts or straps. Children's clothes were similar to adult clothing. Men sometimes wore hide moccasins and leggings, but most of the people were barefoot.

Have you wondered how we can find out what people wore or what their lives were like long ago? Can we travel back through time and take a look? Not yet! The Seminoles and Miccosukees did not pack their clothes in special waterproof trunks or a time capsule so that people like us can look at them today. They usually had to wear their everyday clothes until they wore them out.

We know what the people wore over one hundred years ago by

Photos taken in the late nineteenth and early twentieth century show what men, women, and children wore in those days. The clothing was made of calico (printed cotton) and hand-sewn by the women. Women wore a long skirt with a blouse that had long sleeves and a ruffle on the shoulder. Silver discs were attached to the ruffle. and they wore many strands of bead necklaces. Their hair was pulled up on top of the head in an attractive style with bangs on the forehead.

looking at the many photographs that have been taken of the men, women, and children in their colorful clothing. When we look at pictures, we can see what they wore during different years and see the changes they made. Also, some of the clothing still exists in museums or in private collections, so we can actually see the materials used to make them.

You have probably read about the Seminoles and Miccosukees in history books. Their ancient ancestors were known as Creek Indians. They lived in Georgia and Alabama and began moving into Florida in the eighteenth century. In the nineteenth century the United States fought three wars against the brave Seminole warriors. The government wanted to move the people to "Indian Country," what is now Oklahoma. Present-day Florida Seminoles and Miccosukees are the descendants of the survivors who remained in Florida.

After the wars, the few Indian people left in Florida lived in camps in the south Florida wilderness. Their camps were scattered in the

Everglades, Big Cypress Swamp, and other places, as far away from white people as possible. Toward the end of the nineteenth century, the Indians once more came in contact with white settlers and traders. Traders brought cloth, thread, glass beads, and other supplies to trade with the Indians, in exchange for alligator hides, exotic bird plumes, and animal skins.

Traders introduced an exciting new invention, the hand-cranked sewing machine, and their wives taught the Indian women how to use them. Sewing all of the clothing for a family by hand took a lot of time. The new sewing machines were much quicker to use and inspired the women to create their own unique clothing styles.

Styles of Patchwork Clothing through the Years

Women dressed in long skirts, and the style of the short ruffle on the shoulder of a blouse was changed for a long cape, worn with many pounds of bead necklaces. Yes, pounds!

Men wore a style that became popular in the early 1900s called a "big shirt," a one-piece shirt with a waistband and skirt worn below knee-length. It looks something like a dress to us, but the skirt was more practical for men who spent a lot of time around water and in canoes. They wore one or more scarves tied around the neck.

Both women's skirts and men's big shirts were made of many rows of colorful cloth sewn together, perhaps decorated with a row of **appliqué** design. Appliqué is a cloth decoration made by the sewing technique where cloth is cut, folded, and sewn on top of another piece of cloth.

Non-Indians sometimes make the mistake of calling Native American clothing a "costume." A costume is worn for dress-up or pretend, like for Halloween or to act in a play or movie. But these are the clothes the people wear all the time. They do not call their clothes a costume, just as you probably do not call your jeans, T-shirts, and sneakers a costume. Just as we change our dress styles, they changed their styles over time.

♦ 2 ♦
Twentieth Century

Tourists, Arts and Crafts, and Patchwork Clothing

In the early twentieth century, around 1910, the Seminole and Miccosukee people did fairly well for a short time. They lived in their camps in the wilderness and hunted for alligator hides and exotic bird feathers to trade for cloth and other supplies. However, laws were soon passed to protect the wildlife and they could no longer trade or sell the hides and feathers. The people had to find other ways to make money to survive. Some men took construction or other jobs in the growing cities of Miami and Ft. Lauderdale. In the winter, families would pick tomatoes and other crops for south Florida growers.

Tourists visiting Florida were curious about the Seminole people they had read about and seen in photos in their newspapers up north. They were fascinated by the unusual way they lived in their chickees in the wilderness and traveled in canoes. Exhibition villages opened where tourists could see this interesting lifestyle and the unique clothing of the Indian families living there.

Coppinger's Tropical Gardens, Alligator Farm, and Seminole Indian Village opened on the banks of the Miami River in 1914. Back then, all of the south Florida Native Americans were mostly known to non-Indians as "Seminoles." A rival tourist attraction, Musa Isle Indian Village, opened in 1917. The owners of the villages paid the Indian families to build chickees and live there.

The Indian families worked in the exhibition villages for part of the year and then returned to their camps in the wilderness. They usually were in the exhibition villages during "tourist season," the winter months when it was cold up north and the most tourists came to Florida. The tourist business gave them an opportunity to continue living in their usual way and to earn money to buy cotton cloth, food, supplies, and other things they needed. Children played together and spoke in their native language. Families earned some extra money by making and selling souvenirs.

Do you remember a vacation that you took with your family? Did you bring home a souvenir, something special that makes you remember that trip? Souvenirs are reminders of fun times and interesting places and people. For example, if you visited New York City, you might have bought a glass globe with a little Empire State Building in it, filled with "snow" that swirls around when you shake it. Children who go to Florida on vacation may bring home a Seminole doll as a souvenir.

Seminole women made dolls of red palmetto fiber dressed liked the Indian women to sell in the gift shops. They also made clothing, loomed beadwork belts or bracelets, and wove or coiled baskets to sell. The men carved toy canoes, bows and arrows, and made other souvenirs such as stuffed baby alligators.

Men learned how to wrestle alligators to amuse tourists. Would you want to jump in a pit and wrestle a six-foot alligator? It was exciting to watch and an impressive show. A non-Indian man working in one of the villages showed the Seminoles pictures of totem poles made by Indian tribes in the Northwest Coast. He encouraged the men to carve birds or other animals on wood poles and to paint them in bright colors. They put the poles in front of the villages and inside the grounds to attract and interest tourists.

Tourism became an important business for the Indian people. Some families opened their own camps as exhibition villages and charged for tourists to visit and buy their arts and crafts. Tourism still is an important business for the Seminole and Miccosukee people today.

Around 1917, an Indian woman living in a camp in the south Florida wilderness created the first patchwork design on a hand-cranked sewing machine. Alice Osceola, the wife of William McKinley Osceola (shown here with her daughter Mittie) may have been the first woman to wear a row of patchwork on her dress, such as the fire design seen here (triangles shown on lower sleeve).

Did you ever have a great idea and soon everyone else wanted to do it, too? This idea was the spark that set off a creative explosion. The women call the patchwork "designs," *taweekaache* (tah-wee-GAH-chee) in the language of the Miccosukees. They shared their design ideas with each other.

Think of the bands of the rainbow! That's how their patchwork clothes look. No wonder they are best known for their designs and that the finest art of the Seminoles and Miccosukees in the twentieth century is found in their patchwork clothing.

We go to the mall to buy our ready-made clothes at a store today, and not that many people sew any more, except in factories. There was a time when learning how to make clothes on a sewing machine was considered the most important event in a Seminole or Miccosukee girl's life. Women who make patchwork designs love to tell how they first learned to sew. Girls were usually taught by family members—their mother, aunts, or grandmother, or even by a friend. They learned by watching the other women sew and then practiced when they got a turn on a sewing machine.

Patchwork designs are made by sewing two or more pieces of bright-colored cloth together to make long rows of designs. The cloth first is torn, not cut, into long strips that are sewn together. The strips are cut with sharp scissors and sewn together, then cut and sewn as many times as needed to create a row of the design. This is very hard to do and takes a lot of time. A woman would first spend many hours sewing the rows of designs. Rows of designs are joined to other wide and narrow bands of solid-colored cloth to make clothing.

When tourists and photographers visited the exhibition villages in Miami, they took photos of the families who lived there, wearing their beautiful clothes. Around the year 1920, the photos showed only one or two rows of early patchwork designs sewn among many wide and narrow bands of solid-colored cloth.

The two earliest patchwork designs, rain and fire, were large and boldly colored. One design is made by sewing alternating rectangular strips of two colors of cloth together. It was given the name "rain" when the women were later asked to give "looks-like" names to the designs to easily identify them. Another early design is made of rectangular strips of two colors of cloth that are sewn together and then cut on an angle and sewn again. This saw-tooth design was called "fire" because it looks like leaping flames. "Lightning" and "storm" are other early designs with names inspired by weather. Several designs such as these are so popular that they have been used ever since they were created.

Cross and arrow designs were created. The cross designs come from very ancient Native American religious beliefs and represent the four

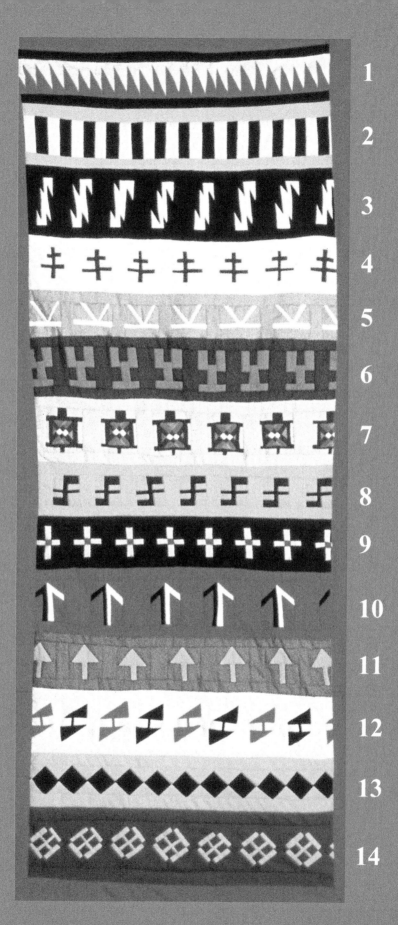

1

2

3

4

5

6

7

8

9

10

11

12

13

14

Patchwork Sampler

Many traditional Seminole patchwork designs have "looks-like" names. In this sampler, created by Effie Osceola, the following designs are portrayed:

1. Fire

2. Rain

3. Lightning

4. Tree or telephone pole

5. Bird flying

6. Crawdad

7. Turtle

8. Man-on-horseback

9. Cross logs of the sacred fire

10. Arrow

11. Arrow

12. Broken arrow

13. Snake or alligator

14. Human bones

directions. A cross with a square in the center represents a sacred fire with logs pointing to the south, east, north, and west. Arrow designs are made several ways. A broken arrow design reminds the people of treaties the United States government made with the Indians that were broken.

Look around you and see what things might inspire a design. Women often took design ideas from things they saw around the camp, like letters of the alphabet copied from boxes, bags, or other containers. It is not known if the letters were copied because they were fun to look at or if the few people who had learned how to read at the time knew their meaning. A, F, H, I, K, L, Y, and X were repeated in rows of designs. T was used both right side up and upside down.

Women created animal designs inspired by the people's oldest nature stories and myths. Designs were created from the legends of crawdad, turtle, and other animals. A "man-on-horseback" design became popular as the people became more involved in raising cattle. Large and small diamond designs are called alligator or diamondback rattlesnake designs.

Deaconess Harriet M. Bedell, an Episcopalian missionary, went to the Glade Cross Mission in 1933 to work with the Indians. She helped them improve the quality of their work and sell their arts and crafts. She encouraged the women to be more productive, to make patchwork clothing and dolls, and to weave or coil more baskets to sell as souvenirs. She expected good design and well-made crafts and found new places and ways to sell them. In 1941, she wrote, "Each woman has a sewing machine and the designs in their costumes are works of art. The designs do not mean anything but are suggestive of running water, a horse's mane, lightning, etc. . . . The women and girls make dolls from palmetto fiber, baskets, and other novelties."

The high point of Seminole and Miccosukee clothing styles was in the 1930s and 1940s. Women's skirts and men's big shirts had as many as five or more rows of tiny patchwork designs. The smaller designs were more difficult to sew and sometimes more than two colors were used in them. Many colors were sometimes used for the body of the clothing and rows of rickrack in different colors were sewn on the cloth. This kaleidoscope of colors is dazzling to see.

The women looked very distinguished in their beautiful outfits. Count the rows of patchwork! They wore a blouse covered by a long cape made of a sheer fabric. The full cape flowed into the line of the skirt. They wore many bead necklaces, which made the neck look long and elegant.

They wore distinctive hairstyles. To create the dramatic hairstyles of the 1940s, the women pulled their hair forward to the front of the head. It was arranged over a half-moon-shaped frame covered with black cloth, all held in place by a hairnet. This served as a sunshade as well.

Men wore shoes and trousers to work at jobs in the city and tucked in the "skirt" of their big shirt. Women designed a "transitional shirt," with a skirt that was made only of several rows of colored cloth and without any patchwork designs. When the skirt was not needed at all because the men wore trousers most of the time, they created a jacket style with a round neck worn with a scarf. In the 1940s, a collar was added to the jacket and it was worn with a shirt bought at a store.

In the 1960s, the women made a lot of patchwork clothing to sell to earn the money they needed. They created new designs made of small rectangular and square pieces forming double diamonds that meet in the center of an X. These designs are rather easy to learn how to make. Easy designs made the same way can be made to look very different from each other by choosing different colors in light and dark shades. Many rows of these similar designs were used in skirts and jackets.

After the Seminole Tribe of Florida and the Miccosukee Tribe of Indians were made official in the mid–twentieth century, leaders of both tribes began to organize their own governments. The tribes built office buildings, and as the women and men took jobs in the offices, they needed suitable clothing styles to wear to work. The women began wearing short patchwork skirts with a blouse or T-shirt and comfortable shoes. Men wore trousers, store-bought shirts, and a jacket or the new vest styles.

Beginning in the 1970s, some women learned how to make very complex wide designs by watching shows about quilting on Miami television stations. Quilting is a technique of sewing pieces of cloth together to make large designs usually used for bed covering. The designs are made by sewing and cutting again and again, sewing many tiny squares of cloth together. Big square quilt designs are joined together square to square. Indian women turn each square design on its point, forming a diamond. The cloth between the diamonds is outlined with many rows of rickrack. Usually only one row of a big design is used for Indian women's long or short skirts.

Solid-colored cloth is usually used for the patchwork. Both solid colors and printed cloth were used between the rows of designs. Women began to use bold prints and expensive special materials such as brocade, shiny satin, or a metallic cloth called lamé.

The women became very creative and careful about choosing their color combinations. Solid colors that coordinate with the other materials and rickrack are selected for the designs. Combinations selected for the solid color or printed cloth between the designs can be very vibrant, using bright colors and prints. Monochromatic combinations—which means all shades of one color—or earth tones such as beige and brown are more conservative.

Clan animals such as Bird, Deer, Bear, Otter, and Panther inspired

new designs created in the 1990s. Seminoles and Miccosukees belong to their mother's "**clan**," a group of related people all descended from a common female ancestor. They named their clans after animals.

The women sew their finest clothing for their families for the annual Green Corn Dance, a religious ceremony that lasts four days and four nights. That is a time of renewal that brings all of the clans together. It is a very special dress-up family occasion where the people honor the **Breathmaker**, the Creator of all things. This event is only for the Seminole and Miccosukee people. It is held in late May or early June, on dates set by the medicine man, a religious leader. Each family member needs several outfits to wear for the many events.

Women make long skirts using shiny cloth that glows in the firelight for the all-night dancing. Their capes are made of lace or other expensive materials. Younger women wear short skirts and a blouse or T-shirt for some of the more active events like the ball game that they play against the men during the day.

Most men wear fancy jackets or vests. Some wear the old-style plain shirt and a doctor's coat, or a big shirt. They wear this with a turban and other accessories like the ones men wore in the nineteenth century.

The twentieth century was a time of great changes but also a very creative time for the Seminole and Miccosukee people. Most of all, they showed their determination to keep their cultural heritage alive.

Clans

Nothing is more important to us than our family. Seminoles and Miccosukees identify their family ties through clans. When babies are born, they become members of their mother's clan. The people are matrilineal, meaning they are descended through the mothers ("matri") in the family's bloodline ("lineal"). Families trace their heritage from mother, grandmother, great-grandmother, and so on. A clan includes other relatives such as aunts, uncles, cousins, and even more distant relatives. Fathers in the camp are originally from other camps, and they are proud of their clans, too. They know the ways and stories of their own clan. So a clan-related uncle, a mother's brother, tells the children the things they need to know about their clan

The people believe that their family clans began long, long ago, when Breathmaker, or Creator, first made the earth and then all of the animals. After they took their place on earth, Breathmaker put them in family groups, clans. There are Bird, Panther, Bear, Otter, Deer, Snake, and other clans. There was a

clan named for Breathmaker's special helper with creation, Wind, the very air we breathe.

Next Breathmaker made humans. At that time, animals and humans could talk to each other and lived together in peace. Coming together as friends, the first human family of each clan began.

The Green Corn Dance

Once a year in May or June, depending on the phase of the new corn moon, the Seminoles and Miccosukees honor Breathmaker for his creation of all new things. It is a celebration that lasts four days and nights with important ritual events, celebration, good food, and family fun. The women sew for weeks to have the beautiful patchwork outfits ready.

The medicine man, the religious leader, decides exactly when the event will be held. People from different clans gather together on a special ceremonial campground in the wilderness. Each clan has its own chickees and responsibilities for the ceremonies. The medicine man and his helpers bring out the soft deerskin bundle that holds "medicine," the mystical animal, plant, and mineral materials that are important to assure the future success and prosperity of the people.

Court is held to settle disagreements or problems. Couples announce their marriages, and boys are given their new adult name at the proper time. Rough-and-tumble stick-ball games are played, with men against the women or boys against the girls.

Everyone dresses in his or her most beautiful new clothes and dances around the fire in a swirl of colors on the last night. Women wear rattles made of turtle shells or tin cans filled with pebbles, attached to a piece of leather wrapped and tied around their legs under their long

skirts. The rattles make a hypnotic shu-shu sound as they dance, a rhythm that puts the dancers in touch with the heartbeat of Mother Earth.

The old sacred fire is put out and a new one lit. Hot coals from the sacred fire are taken home to relight each family campfire. The Green Corn Dance is a time of new beginnings for the people.

A jumble of colors surrounds Effie Osceola as she works on her patchwork. The whirring sound of her sewing machine fills the air. On her table are rows of brilliant patchwork designs she has made, many bolts of different colors of cotton cloth, and big spools of colored thread or rickrack. **Rickrack** is a commercially made saw-tooth decorative trim that is sewn on the cloth between the designs. Bolts, or rolls, of new cotton cloth in bright solid colors are chosen to make patchwork designs. Think of all the colors you know. They are all used: red, blue, yellow, green, bright pink, turquoise, purple, black, white, and many more.

♦ 3 ♦
Twenty-First Century
A Bright Future

Leaders of both the Seminole and Miccosukee tribes have made many positive and progressive decisions to improve the economy of their people. Both tribes are making a lot of money from tourism and other successful businesses. The money is used to improve housing, health care, schools, and offer educational opportunities for the people. Each person registered with the tribes receives money from profits made by tribal businesses.

Although the future looks bright for the people, they are worried about the future of patchwork making. As their lifestyle has changed rapidly, they realize that patchwork still identifies the Seminole and Miccosukee people and that it is a solid link to their past. Many of the women who have sewn are old and they are not sewing anymore. For some, their eyesight is not as good as it once was, so it is more difficult to sew. Few younger women are interested in sewing because they can get better jobs that they think are more interesting, pay more money, and they can have more fun working around other people. Since the patchwork clothing has become very expensive to buy, the people often just wear casual clothing bought at local stores for daily wear. Patchwork outfits are still worn on special occasions.

Girls are encouraged to learn to sew and do beadwork in the Miccosukee school. Classes in making patchwork and other crafts are also taught on Seminole reservations. These culture programs are very important to the survival of the art of making patchwork.

You can see rows of eye-dazzling patchwork clothing and other crafts for sale and meet the people at special events held on the

reservations. The Seminoles host the Seminole Tribal Fair, Powwow, and Rodeo every year in the second week of February on the Hollywood reservation. Native American people come from all over North America to sell their arts and crafts or dance in the powwow at the festival. For many years, this popular event was held in an outdoor stadium on the

Hollywood reservation. The stadium was torn down in 2003, and the tribe built a 279-million-dollar Hard Rock Resort Hotel and Casino on the land. This opened in 2004, and festivals are now held there.

The Clothing Competition has been the most impressive event in the Seminole art festival for over thirty years. Seminole men, women, and children of all ages compete for prize money in contests, wearing clothing in the different styles created over time. Girls and boys wear outfits created for them by their mothers or grandmothers, and it is a beautiful sight to see.

In 1997, the Seminole Tribe opened the Ah-Tah-Thi-Ki Museum, (which means "A Place to Learn, A Place to Remember") that you can visit on the Big Cypress Reservation. This high-tech museum tells the story of their people and how proud they are of their history and culture. Billie Swamp Safari, an ecotourism resort and campground, is nearby. At night, you can listen to Seminoles tell tribal stories by a campfire. The tribe also is opening a new museum at the resort on the Hollywood reservation, which is more convenient for tourists to visit.

The annual Miccosukee Art Festival is held each year from December 26th to January 1st at the Miccosukee Culture Center on the reservation along Tamiami Trail. You can see Miccosukees model their best outfits in a fashion show at the festival, and you can also visit their museum. Arts, crafts, and special Indian foods such as frog legs, "gator bites," Indian tacos, fry bread, and pumpkin fry bread are sold in booths at both Seminole and Miccosukee festivals. The Miccosukees also built an impressive resort hotel and casino at the intersection of the Tamiami Trail and Krome Avenue, not far from their reservation.

Sewing patchwork and making crafts still is important to the Seminole and Miccosukee artists. The artists are proud of their work and you can ask them to explain or demonstrate how they make their beautiful arts and crafts at the special events. There are many things to buy, including patchwork clothing, dolls, beadwork, baskets, drums,

rattles, or carved wood bows and arrows, canoe models, and alligators.

While at these events on the reservation, you will see that the Seminole and Miccosukee children like many of the same things that you like. They play games, ride bikes, and enjoy sports. They like hamburgers and French fries. Most of them live in new modern houses, but the family may still have a chickee near the house to use for storage, extra work space, or for family gatherings.

The children go to new modern schools on the reservations built and managed by the tribes. There are computers and other electronic equipment in their classrooms and they have lots of sports and other activities. They often wear sneakers, shorts or jeans, and T-shirts. Like you, though, they dress up for special occasions and they are proud to wear their patchwork clothing.

Miccosukee Virginia Poole said, "I think our patchwork sets us apart from other tribes. I don't believe any other tribe in the U.S. has the patchwork like the Seminoles and Miccosukees. To me, it's everyday dress. Some of the younger people, they dress in jeans and wear little shirts, but they try to put some patchwork on themselves. To me, it identifies us. I am Indian. I am proud to be an Indian. It's my heritage."

You have learned a lot about the Seminole and Miccosukee Indian people. You have seen how creative they were in the nineteenth and twentieth centuries, in spite of difficulties. They are modern, progressive, and successful in the twenty-first century. Not only that, you know that clothes can be art! Now have fun with the art activities of making patchwork designs and a doll with a row of fire patchwork on her skirt.

◆ 4 ◆
Art Activities

Let's Make Patchwork Designs and a Doll

Let's make some patchwork designs and samples. You know that Seminole and Miccosukee patchwork designs are made with cloth sewn on a sewing machine. You may not have a sewing machine because most of us today buy our clothes ready-made from a store. To create designs that look like patchwork, you use crayons or markers or colored construction paper instead of cloth, and glue instead of needle and thread. If these activities are done in a classroom or with adult supervision, it would be easiest to use a paper cutter for several of these activities so that many strips of paper could be cut at one time.

You will still learn important things about making patchwork designs. You will notice that the designs are always straight lines, no curves. One design, done in the same color combination, is repeated over and over again in a long row. You will learn about color selection and color values (shades of one color from light to dark). You will see how much work it takes to make patchwork designs.

Sampler of Rain, Fire, and Storm Designs

Materials
- Colored construction paper, 9 x 12 inches
- White construction paper, 9 x 12 inches
- Ruler, Pencil, Scissors, Glue, Black ink pen

For the sampler background, select a sheet of construction paper. You will glue on three examples of patchwork designs: rain, fire, and storm. At the left of each design on the sampler is a piece that shows how it was made.

Rain Design

1. Select two different colors of construction paper. Use a ruler and pencil to measure and use scissors to cut a strip in each color, 1 inch wide x 12 inches long. (You can cut the entire length of 12 inches, but you won't use it all.)
2. Cut a strip of white construction paper, 2 inches wide x 12 inches long.
3. Glue the two colored strips side by side onto the white strip (a).

a.

4. Cut a 2-inch wide piece of this and glue it onto your background piece in the upper left corner (see sampler).
5. Cut the rest of the strip every 2 inches to make pieces (b).

b.

6. Turn pieces vertically, alternating colors, and glue these onto the second white strip (c).
7. Glue some of this strip of rain design onto your background piece in the top right corner (see sampler).

c.

Fire Design

1. Select two different colors of construction paper. Cut a strip in each color, 1 inch wide x 12 inches long, as above.
2. Cut three strips of white construction paper, 2 inches wide x 12 inches long.
3. Glue the two colored strips side by side onto one of the white strips.
4. Cut the colored strips into 2-inch-wide pieces, as above.
5. Turn the pieces vertically, alternating colors, and glue them onto the second white strip. You should now have a row that looks like rain design.

a.

6. Use a black pen to draw dark lines at an angle across the pieces to show how it will be cut (a).

b.

8. Cut off and glue two of these pieces onto your background piece, on the left side of the middle row (see sampler).
9. Cut the rest of the pieces apart and cut them diagonally on the dark lines you drew (b).

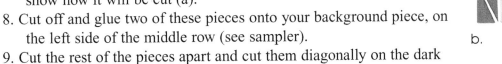

c.

10. Now make the fire design by gluing the triangles you just cut onto the third white strip, alternating colors, alternating pointed ends (c).
11. Glue some of this row of fire design onto your background piece, on the right side of the middle row (see sampler).

Storm Design

1. Select two different colors of construction paper. Cut a strip of each color, 2 inches wide x 12 inches long.

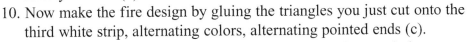

a.

2. Cut two strips of white construction paper, 4 inches wide x 12 inches long.
3. Glue the colored strips side by side onto one white strip (a).

b.

4. Cut colored pieces, 1 inch wide x 4 inches high, from the two-color strip (b).

5. Glue one piece onto your background piece, in the bottom left corner (see sampler).
6. Glue the rest of the pieces to the other white strip, turning the pieces up and down, alternating the color to make a row of storm design (c).

c.

7. Glue some of this strip of storm design onto your background piece in the bottom right corner (see sampler).

Row of Patchwork

Materials
• 6 colors of construction paper, 9 x 12 inches
• 1 piece white construction paper, 9 x 12 inches
• 1 piece white paper, 8 1/2 x 11 inches
• Pencil, Ruler, Scissors, Glue, Black ink pen

The photograph to the right shows what the finished patchwork sampler should look like. Figures a–f will show you how each step should look when you have completed it.

1. Select three different colors of construction paper. Use a ruler and pencil to measure and use scissors to cut one strip of each color, 1 inch wide by 12 inches long. (You can cut the entire length of 12 inches, but you may not use it all.)

a.

2. Cut one strip of white construction paper, 3 inches wide x 12 inches long.

b.

3. Glue the strips of colored construction paper side by side onto the white strip. You should now have one tri-colored strip.
4. Cut one 3-inch-wide piece from the tri-colored strip (a).
5. Draw two black lines, 1 inch apart, on the 3-inch-wide tri-colored piece (b).

c.

6. Cut the strip along the lines you drew, so that you have three 1-inch-wide pieces.
7. Glue these pieces on the white paper in "stair steps" (c). Trim away the white paper.

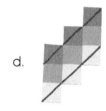

8. Draw a line on the stair steps across the diamonds on the top and bottom (d).

d.

9. Cut the stair steps across the lines that you drew (e). This will be your row of patchwork.

e.

10. From the piece of different-colored construction paper, use a ruler and pencil to measure a 6-inch square. Cut it out.

11. Glue your row of patchwork in the center of the square (f).
12. Think colorful! Select another color of paper and cut a strip 1/2 inch wide x 12 inches long. Cut it in half to make two 6-inch-long strips. Glue them on the square above and below your row of patchwork. Make sure you leave space between them so the color of the construction paper square shows through.

f.

13. Select another color of paper and cut a strip 1/2 inch wide x 12 inches long. Cut it in half to make two 6-inch-long strips. Glue one strip 1/2 inch from the top of the square, and the other 1/2 inch from the bottom.

If you want to try this again, use different colors to see how they change the way your design looks.

X Designs
Explore Colors and Color Values

In the 1960s, Seminole and Miccosukee women made designs based on an X that were easy to learn to make. The designs could be made to look different from each other just by changing the colors and arrangement of color values. The color value is the shading of one color from light to dark, such as from pale pink to dark red.

Choosing Colors
The women usually choose very bright solid-colored cotton cloth to make designs. They may pick warm colors like red and yellow, or cool colors like green and blue. Turquoise, purple, pink, and orange also are popular. There are so many colors to choose from!

Color Values
Contrast of color values is important, too. Different shades of a color appear to move toward you or away from you. Take a piece of white and black paper and hold them up in front of you. Which seems closer to you and which seems farther away? White and light colors seem to move toward you, while black or dark colors move away from you. These differences change the way a design looks.

Now you are going to use the patterns to experiment with some X designs. Look at the illustrations of examples of different X designs and some ways they can be made using color value variations.

Materials
- Design patterns on next page
- a copy machine
- White or black construction paper to be used as a background
- Colored markers or crayons
        or
  Several colors of construction paper, ruler, pencil, scissors, glue

Directions
1. Copy the patterns
2. Carefully choose the colors and color values you want to use. Look at the examples and decide how many colors you want to use for each design. Remember to use contrasting light and dark values. The white paper of the pattern can also be used as a color.
3. *Using crayons or colored markers*
    Experiment using different colors on a piece of white paper before you make your color selections.
    Using pieces of colored construction paper
    Cut pieces of selected colors to fit sizes on the pattern. Start with the bigger rectangles or squares, then the middle strips, finally the center X squares. Glue the pieces on starting either with the large pieces at the outer edges or with the small center pieces. When you finish, draw a straight line around all four edges and trim.
4. Glue to a background of black or white construction paper to display all the X designs you have made.

Different ways one design can look

Different X designs

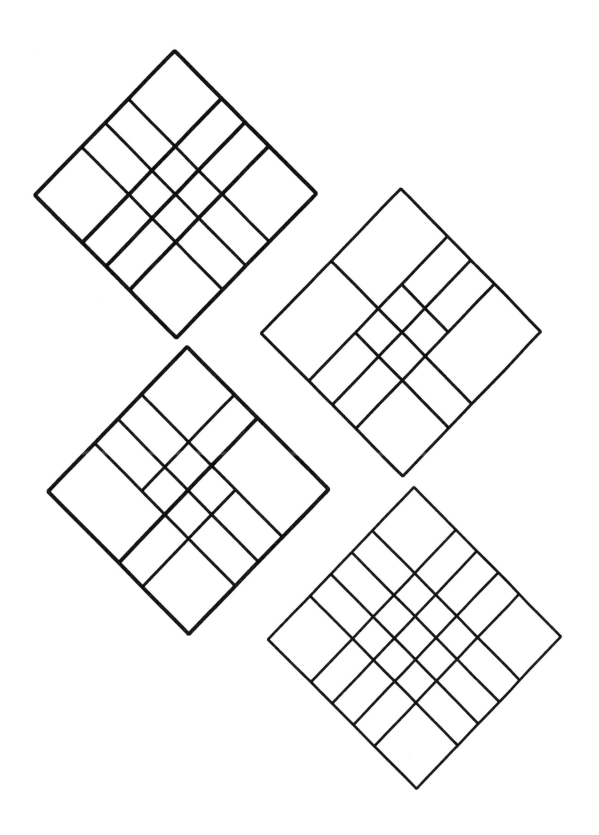

Animal Design

Look at some of the animals designs shown in photos in this book, such as turtle, crawdad, deer, bird flying, and others. Some designs, like deer or panther, are more realistic or natural. Other designs, like crawdad and turtle, are more abstract, which means the animal is not represented realistically. One design, bear, just suggests the thought of a bear by representing a bear's paw. Notice that all of these animals are made with straight lines, no curves. Even the panther's tail is made with straight lines. You can create your own animal designs.

Materials
- Photos of animals from magazines
- Colored construction paper
- White paper, Ruler, Pencil, Scissors, Glue

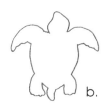

a.

Directions
1. Choose a small picture of an animal from a magazine, or draw one, and cut it out. If you find a picture that is too big or too small, you can change the size on a copy machine (a and b).
2. Draw the animal's shape on white paper. Use a ruler to straighten out the curves (c). Cut it out with scissors.
3. Put it on construction paper and trace around it. Cut it out. You can cut more than one at once by folding the paper.
4. Cut a strip of different-colored construction paper wide and long enough for your animal.
5. Glue the animal designs in a row.

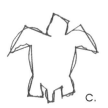

b.

c.

Sampler of Designs

This sampler shows some Miccosukee patchwork designs. They have "looks-like" names such as lightning and crawdad. Effie Osceola, a talented artist, created the bird flying design for this sampler.

Copy the pattern of the sampler on a copy machine one or more times. Choose any colors that you like. Then color each row of designs. Remember to use the same colors for the whole row of the design. Add your own design for the bottom row.

My Sampler of Designs

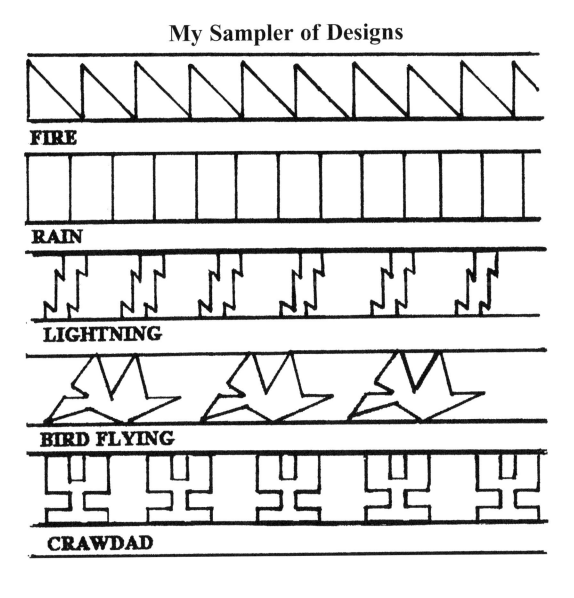

FIRE

RAIN

LIGHTNING

BIRD FLYING

CRAWDAD

MY DESIGN

Doll

Seminole Indian dolls have been sold to tourists since the early 1900s and they are some of the best known of all Native American dolls. They are still popular souvenirs today, bought by both tourists and art collectors. Most dolls are made to represent women, but some dolls are made to represent men. The female dolls have a fancy hairstyle, a red mouth, and bright black and white eyes. They are dressed in the traditional style, wearing a colorful cape and skirt and hairstyles similar to what the Native American women used to wear. The cape and skirt are decorated with rickrack and a row of patchwork is sewn on the skirts of some dolls.

Dolls are made of palmetto fiber, the "husk" of the palmetto. It is reddish-brown, a color the Seminole and Miccosukee people think to be appropriate for dolls representing Indian people. The body is covered by the skirt and cape and is made without either arms or legs. Many rows of rickrack are sewn on the cloth.

Black cloth or yarn representing traditional hairstyles is added to the head. To recreate the elaborate hairstyle of the 1940s, the doll's head is covered with black cloth, which is then pulled over a half-moon cardboard frame. A more modern ponytail was a popular hairstyle for both the women and the dolls in the late 1950s. Black silk or wool yarn is used to make this style. Two braids made of black wool yarn represent another favorite hairstyle for dolls.

Materials
- Copy Machine
- Empty toilet paper roll
- 2 tissues (like Kleenex ™)
- Brightly colored tissue paper
- Brown tissue paper
- Black tissue paper
- Black, brown, and brightly colored construction paper, 9 x 12 inches
- One 12-inch piece of rickrack
- White, red, and black colored pencils
- Colored pony beads or large seed beads
- Small-gauge craft wire or fishing line
- Ruler, Pencil, Scissors, Glue, Stapler, Clear tape

Copy the Doll Patterns from page 51 for the patchwork, face, and hair frame.

Body
1. Cut a piece of brown construction paper, 4 1/2 inches long x 6 inches wide.
2. Glue it to the toilet paper roll. Let it dry.

Skirt
1. Select a piece of brightly colored construction paper. Cut a piece 4 inches wide x 12 inches long.
2. To make a row of patchwork with a fire design on it, select two contrasting colors of construction paper and cut a strip, 1/2 inch wide x 12 inches long, from each one.
3. Cut out the pattern for the fire design. Be careful not to cut all the way through the bottom of the design.
4. Using a small piece of clear tape, put the pattern on one of the colored strips. Use a pencil to trace the design onto the construction paper. Repeat this process, moving the pattern down the strip until you reach the end.
5. Use scissors to cut the design out of the construction paper. Be careful not to cut all the way through the bottom of it.
6. Put glue on the side of the design that has pencil lines on it, and glue it to the other, uncut, strip of construction paper. This is your fire design.
7. Glue the design just above the bottom of the skirt.
8. Select a fourth color of construction paper and cut a strip 1/2 inch wide x 12 inches long. Glue as the top row of the skirt, 1/2 inch above the row of fire design (a). Let dry.

a.

Cape
1. Cut a piece of brightly colored tissue paper, 6 inches wide x 12 inches long.
2. Fold in half so that it is 3 inch wide x 12 inches long. The folded edge is the bottom of the cape.
3. Above the bottom of the folded edge, glue a 12-inch piece of rickrack (b).

b.

Head and Hair
1. Cut out the pattern for the face. Wad two tissues into a ball, 1 1/2 inches in diameter (about the size of the pattern).
2. Cut out two sheets of brown tissue paper, 7 inches square. Use one to cover the tissue head. Tie it at the neck with the craft wire or fishing line.
3. Put the face pattern against the head where the face will be drawn and place the other piece of brown tissue paper over the head (c).

c.

4. Use colored pencils to draw the face over the pattern. First draw a straight line in red for the mouth. Then draw two white horizontal lines for the eyes, and draw one black vertical line in the center of each for the pupils.
5. Cut out a sheet of black tissue paper, 6 inches square, and fold it in half. Glue it to the back of the head. (To see what this should look like from the side, see d.)

d.

6. Cut out the pattern for the hair frame.
7. Use a pencil to trace it onto a piece of black construction paper, and cut it out with scissors.

Assembly
1. To assemble the head and body, pinch in both sides of one end of the toilet paper roll. This will be the top of the doll. Holding the head, put glue on the outside of the neck and place it inside the pinched opening of the body. Tape and then staple the sides of the pinched body to hold the head (e).
2. Gather several folds in the top of the skirt and staple them.
3. Slide the skirt onto the body, covering the bottom of the paper roll. Glue and staple the edges, and tape it to the body.
4. Gather the cape at the top and staple around the neck with the opening in back. Glue the sides of the opening together.
5. To make a necklace, use a piece of wire or fishing line that is long enough to wrap around the doll's neck more than twice. String one bead on the wire or fishing line and tie a knot around the bead. Push the wire or fishing line through the bead again, then string enough beads to make several rows of a necklace. Tie a knot around the last bead and knot the ends. Put on the doll around her neck.
6. Glue the hair frame to the brown tissue paper of the face, near the black tissue paper of the hair. Curve it slightly. Let dry.
7. Glue one larger bead or a tiny gold ring to each side of the hair frame to make earrings.

e.

Doll Patterns

Fire Design for Skirt

Face Pattern

Hair Frame Pattern

Glossary

appliqué: a cut, folded, and sewn cloth decoration.

Breathmaker: an English word Seminoles and Miccosukees use to refer to Creator or God.

chickee: an open-sided house or building with a palmetto-thatched roof.

clan: a group of families that claim to be descended from a common ancestor.

Miccosukee: a word used for the people and language of the Miccosukee Tribe of Indians of Florida.

Mikasuki: a Native American language spoken by members of the Seminole Tribe of Florida who live on the Hollywood, Big Cypress, Immokalee, and the smaller Tampa and Ft. Pierce reservations.

patchwork: designs made by sewing pieces of colored cloth together.

reservation: land set aside by the United States government for Native American people to live on or to use for special purposes.

rickrack: a commercially made saw-tooth decorative trim.

Seminole: a Native American tribe, descended from the Creeks, whose members live in both Florida and Oklahoma.

sofke: Miccosukee word for a warm drink made of water and ground corn.

turban: a headdress made of cloth wrapped around the head.

Suggested Reading

Downs, Dorothy. *Art of the Florida Seminole and Miccosukee Indians.* Gainesville, Florida: University Press of Florida, 1995.

Jumper, Betty Mae. *Legends of the Seminoles.* Sarasota, Florida: Pineapple Press, 1994.

Kersey, Harry A., Jr. *Pelts, Plumes, and Hides.* Gainesville, Florida: University Presses of Florida, 1975.

Lourie, Peter. *Everglades: Buffalo Tiger and the River of Grass.* Honesdale, Pennsylvania: Boyds Mills Press, Inc.,1994.

McCarthy, Kevin M. *Native Americans in Florida.* Sarasota, Florida: Pineapple Press, 1999.

Rush, Beverly and Wittman, Lassie. *The Complete Book of Seminole Patchwork.* New York: Dover Publishing, 1994.

Weisman, Brent Richards. *Florida's Seminole and Miccosukee Indians.* Gainesville, Florida: University Press of Florida. 1999.

West, Patsy. *The Enduring Seminoles: From Alligator Wrestling to Ecotourism.* Gainesville, Florida: University Press of Florida, 1998.

Acknowledgments

I wish to thank Effie Osceola and Frances Osceola and their families who graciously allowed me to visit their camps, where I spent many hours in their sewing chickees watching them sew beautiful patchwork clothing. Annie Tiger Jim, Mary Frances Johns, and many other friends shared their feelings about how much sewing patchwork means to Seminole and Miccosukee women and girls.

I also wish to thank the teachers who made suggestions for this book, including Linda Harrell, Joanna Lopez, Patricia Tuttle, and Phyllis Walker. Thanks again to Patricia Tuttle for making the beautiful doll on page 50. And thanks to Rowena Luna for her map.

Special thanks go to the patchwork gang at Pineapple Press for their work on the book: to Britt Dienes for her work on the doll, Helena Sznurkowski for her word wizardry, June Cussen for her how-to photography, and Shé Heaton for her wonderful design skills.

Credits

Illustrations by the author unless otherwise noted

Here are some other books from Pineapple Press on related topics. For a complete catalog, visit our website at www.pineapplepress.com. Or write to Pineapple Press, P.O. Box 3889, Sarasota, Florida 34230-3889, or call (800) 746-3275.

Crafts of Florida's First People by Robin Brown. Learn how to throw spears and darts, make pottery, weave cloth, mix paint, build traps, and even how to start a fire without matches—just the way Florida's first people did it for thousands of years. Full color. Ages 10 and up. (pb)

Florida's First People by Robin Brown. Filled with photos of replicas of technologies used by early peoples in their daily lives, this book brings to life the first humans who entered Florida about 12,000 years ago. (hb)

Florida's Fossils by Robin Brown. Includes a complete identification section and insightful comments on the history of the fossil treasures you'll uncover. Amateur archaeologists will appreciate updated maps and directions to some of the best fossil-hunting areas in Florida. (pb)

Native Americans in Florida by Kevin M. McCarthy. Long before the first European explorers set foot on Florida soil, numerous Native American tribes hunted, honored their gods, and build burial mounds. This book explores the importance of preserving the past and how archaeologists do their work. The different types of Indian mounds and their uses are explained, as well as Indian languages and reservations. Ages 10 and up. (hb)

Legends of the Seminoles by Betty Mae Jumper with Peter Gallagher, paintings by Guy LaBree. For the first time, stories and legends handed down through generations by tribal elders have been set down for all to enjoy. Each tale is illustrated with an original color painting. (pb)

My Florida Facts by Russell W. Johnson and Annie P. Johnson, illustrated by Michael Swing. Learn facts about Florida—from the state capital to the number of counties in Florida and much more—through the catchy lyrics of the song "My Florida Facts." Includes a CD with the easily learned song, performed by children. Ages 8–12. (hb)

Florida A to Z by Susan Jane Ryan, illustrated by Carol Tornatore. From Alligator to Zephyrhills, you'll find more information on Florida packed in this alphabet than you can imagine—almost 200 facts about Florida personalities, history, geography, nature, and culture. Full color throughout. Ages 9–12. (hb)

America's REAL First Thanksgiving by Robyn Gioia. When most Americans think of the first Thanksgiving, they think of the Pilgrims and the Indians in New England in 1621. But on September 8, 1565, the Spanish and the native Timucua celebrated with a feast of Thanksgiving in St. Augustine. Teacher's activity guide also available. Ages 9–14. (hb)

The Young Naturalist's Guide to Florida, **Second Edition,** by Peggy Sias Lantz and Wendy A. Hale. Provides up-to-date information about Florida's wonderful natural places and the plants and creatures that live here—many of which are found nowhere else in the United States. Learn about careers in the environmental field and how to help protect Florida's beautiful places. Ages 10–14. (pb)

Everglades: An Ecosystem Facing Choices and Challenges by Anne E. Ake. The shallow, slowly flowing waters of the Everglades create an ecosystem of mysterious beauty with a great diversity of plant and animal life. But it is an ecosystem in trouble. Learn about how the Comprehensive Restoration Plan (CERP) is bringing many groups together to try to save the Everglades. Lots of color photos. Ages 11–14. (hb)

African Americans in Florida by Maxine D. Jones and Kevin McCarthy. Profiles more than fifty African Americans during four centuries of Florida history in brief essays. Traces the role of African Americans played in his discovery, exploration, and settlement of Florida as well as through the Civil War to the Civil Rights movement. Ages 10 and up. (pb)

CPSIA information can be obtained
at www.ICGtesting.com
Printed in the USA
BVOW07s0141201216
471288BV00004B/4/P